731

R01913 L3L04
R06066 27173

WRIGHTWOOD-ASHBURN BRANCH LIBRARY
8498 S. KEDZIE
CHICAGO, ILLINOIS 60652

D1529076

```
DA      Wilkins, Frances.
320
.W5        Growing up in the
             Age of Chivalry

    Cop. 1
```

```
DA      Wilkins, Frances.              95
320
.W5      Growing up in the
             Age of Chivalry

    cop. 1

 MAR  - 1979                        6.95
```

DATE	BORROWER'S NAME	

WRIGHTWOOD BRANCH LIBRARY
2519 WEST 79th STREET
CHICAGO, ILLINOIS 60652

© THE BAKER & TAYLOR CO.

Growing up in
THE AGE OF CHIVALRY

Frances Wilkins

G.P. Putnam's Sons, New York

© Frances Wilkins 1977

First published 1977

ISBN 0-399-20634-5
Library of Congress Catalog Card Number 77-84931

Printed in Great Britain
for the Publishers G. P. Putnam's Sons
200 Madison Avenue, New York 10016

DA
320
.W5

cop. 1

Frontispiece   Miniature portrait of a girl aged 5 by
Isaac Oliver, 1590 (Salting Bequest)

Acknowledgment

Figure 20 is reproduced by the Gracious Permission
of Her Majesty the Queen. The Author and Publishers
also thank the following for their kind permission
to reproduce copyright illustrations: the Bodleian
Library, Oxford, for figs 14 and 46; the Trustees of
British Museum for figs 3 and 17; John Freeman for
fig 48; A.F. Kersting for fig 22; the Mansell Collection
for figs 1, 11, 35, 38, 45, 52, 60 and 61; the
National Portrait Gallery for figs 19, 44, 53 and 59;
the Public Record Office, London, for fig 31; the
Radio Times Hulton Picture Library for figs 4-10,
12, 13, 15, 18, 21, 27-30, 36, 37, 39, 41, 49, 55
and 56; the Victoria and Albert Museum for the
frontispiece and figs 16, 40 and 43. The other
illustrations appearing in the book are the property
of the Publishers.

R01913 62608

Contents

The Illustrations

1 The Tudor Age

The Tudor period, which has been called the Age of Chivalry, lasted for just over one hundred years. It began in 1485 when Henry VII (1456-1509) was declared king after winning the Battle of Bosworth. It included the reigns of Henry VIII (1491-1547), Edward VI (1537-1553) and Mary I (1516-1558), and ended with the death of Elizabeth I (b.1533) in 1603.

All these Tudor monarchs were, to some extent, despots. But most people were pleased to have firm rule at last after the long drawn out conflicts of the previous century. As a result, the country prospered, despite all the great changes and upheavals which were so characteristic of this period in English history.

Voyages of exploration

One very important change was the increase in the size of the known world. When Henry VII came to the throne people knew little or nothing of what lay beyond the countries of Western Europe. Then in 1486 Bartholomew Diaz rounded the Cape of Good Hope, six years later Christopher Columbus reached the West Indies and five years after that John Cabot discovered Newfoundland.

1   Map of the world drawn for the declaration of a discovery. It was thought that the world was flat until the explorers discovered the continent of America. Sir Francis Drake was the first Englishman to sail all the way round the world in 1577.

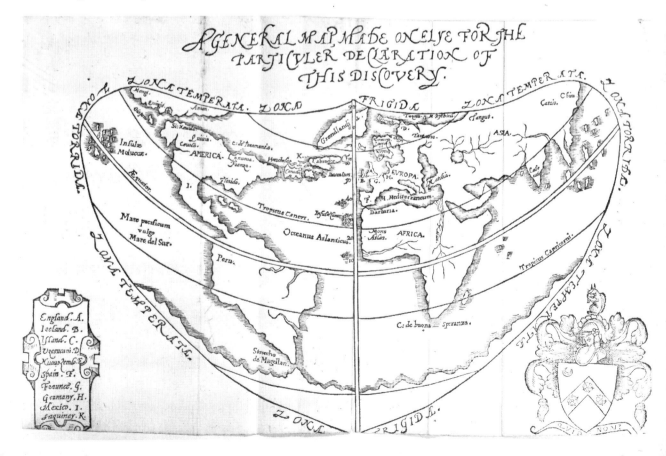

2 Erasmus, the Dutch philosopher, meeting the
children of Henry VII. This painting captures the
spirit of the Renaissance, a time of cultural
expansion and commercial growth. The royal
children are wearing adult fashions, and the baby
is clothed in a stiff embroidered costume with a
tight-fitting cap.

All these early navigators naturally needed tremendous courage. By present-day standards the ships in which they made these long voyages were little more than cockle-shells. They were also venturing into completely uncharted waters, at a time when many people were firmly convinced that if you sailed too far you would fall right over the edge of the world!

All the great maritime nations were determined to establish new trade routes, particularly to India, China, and the other countries in the East. So as soon as the first great navigators had shown the way, all the Western countries began sending ships regularly on long, but usually highly profitable, voyages.

Trade and commerce

The effect in Britain was a dramatic change in the nation's economy. This was no longer based entirely on agriculture, as it had been throughout the whole of the Middle Ages.

Instead trade and commerce became increasingly important, especially the production and export of wool, and a new middle class of prosperous merchants began to emerge.

The change in the economy naturally led to a drift away from the land. When Henry VII came to the throne the population was three million, of whom at least eighty per cent lived and worked in the country. By the end of the Tudor period, on the other hand, although the population had risen to some four million, the number of people engaged in agriculture had sharply declined.

3   Map of Britain in 1590. Scotland did not join the United Kingdom until James I's accession in 1603. The decorative border shows Queen Elizabeth, a nobleman and his wife, and a merchant and his wife. Weapons, books, navigation instruments and lutes are depicted beside the nobility, while crops, sheep, cloth and gold are placed beside the merchant.

The Renaissance

Another great change that took place in Tudor times was in people's attitude to learning. 'I would rather see my son hanged than a scholar', was a typical remark among the rich in early Tudor times. The nobility still thought of themselves as knights and courtly gentlemen, just as their forbears had been in Medieval times, and they looked down their noses at 'clerkly pursuits'.

Nevertheless a change was already taking place. In 1453 the Turks had captured Constantinople, and a great many classical scholars who had been living there had decided to flee to the West. Most of them made their new homes in Italy, bringing with them their knowledge of Ancient Greece and Rome, and of the classical languages, which had been almost entirely

4 A printing house. The boy apprentice is collating the printed pages.

forgotten in the West.

Before long people all over Europe were studying the classics. And this in turn gave rise to a new interest in all forms of learning. This new interest, called the Renaissance, was also given additional impetus by the fact that printing had just been invented, and there was an ever increasing number of books for people to study. Johannes Gutenberg produced the first printed book, the Gutenberg Bible, in Mainz in 1450; in 1477 William Caxton set up the first press in England, in Westminster.

5 A page from Tyndale's 'New Testament', 1525.

The gospell of S. Mathew.
The fyrst Chapter.

Hys ys the boke of the generacio of Jesus Christ the sonne of David/The sonne also of Abraham. Chã.

Abraham begatt Isaac:
Isaac begatt Jacob:
Jacob begatt Judas and hys brethren:
Judas begat Phares:
and Zaram of thamar:
Phares begatt Esrom:
Esrom begatt Aram:
Aram begatt Aminadab:
Aminadab begatt naassan:
Naasson begatt Salmon:
Salmon begatt boos of rahab:
Boos begatt obed of ruth:
Obed begatt Jesse:
Jesse begatt david the kynge:
David the kynge begatt Solomon/of her that was the wyfe of vry:
Solomon begat roboam:
Roboam begatt Abia:
Abia begatt asa:
Asa begatt iosaphat:
Josaphat begatt Joram:
Joram begatt Osias:
Osias begatt Joatham:
Joatham begatt Achas:
Achas begatt Ezechias:
Ezechias begatt Manasses:
Manasses begatt Amon:
Amon begatt Josias:
Josias begatt Jechonias and his brethren about the tyme of the captivite of babilen
After they were led captive to babilen/ Jechonias begatt

Abraham and David are fyrst rehearsid/ because that christe was chefly promysed vnto them.

Saynct mathew leveth out certeyne generacions/ z describeth Christes linage from solomõ/after the lawe of Moses/ but Lucas descrybeth it accordyng to nature/frõ nathan solomõs brother. For the lawe calleth them a mannes childrẽ which his broder begatt of his wyfe lefte behynde hym after his deth. Deu. xxv.c.

9

The Reformation

Closely linked with the Renaissance were the religious changes of Tudor times. As people began to read and study for themselves, many of them began to question the traditional teachings of the Catholic Church. In particular, a great many scholars were reading the New Testament for the first time in the original Greek, and they did not always agree with the Church's interpretation.

In England the immediate cause of the religious changes was political, however. Henry VIII wanted to rule the nation as he pleased, and he also coveted the vast wealth of the Catholic Church in Britain. So in 1529 he declared himself the Head of the Church of England, and made the country entirely independent of the Pope and of Rome.

The Reformation, as it was called, was supported by most of the better educated people. But many of the simple, working people felt lost and bewildered when all the old rituals and customs were swept away. In particular, they missed the monasteries and the nunneries, where they had been used to going for help whenever they were in difficulty or distress.

By Elizabeth's reign, however, the new religion was firmly established. The Bible had been translated into English, and the Book of Common Prayer was in use in all the churches. Any lingering opposition to the Church of England finally came to an end in 1588 when the whole nation united to defeat the Spanish Armada, which was aimed at restoring the Catholic religion in England.

The end of the Middle Ages

The Tudor period is often described as a turning-point in English history. The reason is that it marks the end of the Middle Ages and the beginning of Modern times. This makes it one of the most exciting and challenging times there has ever been for a child to grow up in.

6   Henry VIII and his son Edward VI.

2 Young Noblemen

Paintings of children in Tudor times hand on the walls of many stately homes, and are reproduced in a great many history books. But the children in these paintings are not typical of the boys and girls at that period. They are all the sons and daughters of very wealthy people, who could afford to have their children painted.

In Tudor times there were four quite separate social classes. First, there were the very wealthy, who did not make up more than about five per cent of the population. Then there was the rapidly expanding group of well-to-do merchants and traders. Thirdly, there were the comfortably-off yeomen. And lastly, by far the largest group of all, there were the poor.

All these different classes of people lived strikingly different lives. Even as children they would have had very little in common with each other. So there is only one way to get a true picture of what it was like to grow up in Tudor times. This is to look at the children in each of these four groups in turn.

Let us begin with the boys whose portraits hang in the stately homes. (We will consider the girls later, as, once again, their lives were quite different from the lives of their brothers.) We do, in fact, know more about these boys than we do about the children in the other groups. This is because it was mainly the rich who kept diaries and household accounts and wrote letters, which can still be read today.

Miniature adults

The most striking fact about these rich boys is that they were always treated as adults. Even quite tiny children were just regarded as small (rather troublesome!) grown-ups. The good boy was the one who was most like an adult in his behaviour. It never occurred to anyone that boys might have different interests and aptitudes from their fathers.

The greatest compliment you could pay to a boy was to say that he was like a man. For instance, you may have heard of Sir Philip Sidney (1554-1586), the famous Elizabethan poet and courtier. (It was Sir Philip Sidney who refused a drink of water when he was dying on the battlefield, saying that another wounded soldier had a greater need of the water than he had.) Writing in praise of Sir Philip Sidney when he was a boy, one of his friends said, 'Though I knew him from a child, yet I never knew him to be other than a man. He possessed such staidness of mind, such lovely and familiar gravity, as carried a grace and reverence far beyond his years'.

Since boys were regarded as small adults it followed that they were dressed like adults. No allowance at all was made for the fact that they might want to run about and play. In Henry VIII's reign boys wore several layers of loose garments. They had a shirt, doublet, jerkin and gown on the upper half of the body, and loose breeches and stockings on the legs. By Queen Elizabeth's

7 Sir Walter Raleigh and his son, 1602. The boy dresses and poses exactly like his father.

time these loose clothes had given way to elaborate, tightly padded garments. The padded doublets had high, starched ruffs, and the breeches were also thickly padded, and slashed. Perhaps this is the reason Tudor boys did not mind sitting on hard wooden seats. They were carrying their own cushions around with them, inside their breeches!

Education: Pages

All through the Tudor period a rich boy received his first lessons at home. He had a tutor to teach him to read and write and to do simple arithmetic. Most of the work was done orally, with the tutor reciting the lesson first, and the boys then repeating it after him, as there were no special books for small children in those days.

At the age of seven or eight a boy's serious education began. As might be expected, ideas on education were much the same as ideas on dress. The principal aim was to make a boy think and behave like a man at the earliest possible age. But views on what was expected of a nobleman changed considerably during the course of the Tudor period.

In early Tudor times the emphasis was on social accomplishments. It was not thought necessary for a nobleman to have a great deal of academic learning. As one rich landowner said, 'I would rather see my son hanged than a bookworm. It is a gentleman's calling to be able to blow the horn, to hunt and to hawk. A gentleman should leave learning to clodhoppers'.

Oddly enough, it was not thought that a boy could learn these social graces at home. Instead he was usually sent as a page to some other nobleman's household. This meant that he became a kind of personal servant to the nobleman. He waited on him at table, and accompanied him whenever he went out. In this way it was hoped that he would learn to copy the nobleman 'in all the actions of his life, whether connected with the institution of a nobleman or with

8 A nobleman's education trained him for war. A battle such as this (Pinkie, 1547) provided valuable opportunities to win glory and honours.

the wars', as one writer expressed it. In other words, he would learn how to hunt and to hawk, to joust and to fence, to play the lute and, if necessary, to fight bravely in battle.

Education: Scholars

By late Tudor times this was not considered enough, however. More and more stress was being placed on the need for an academic education. In fact, one group of boys was warned, 'You will do your prince poor service, you will stand your country in poor stead, and you will bring yourselves but small preferment, if you be no scholars'.

One reason for the change was the growing importance of trade and commerce. Every day more and more boys from ordinary middle-class homes were entering the newly founded grammar schools. Many of these boys were later becoming wealthy merchants and bankers. As a result, most of the noblemen were slowly coming to realize that if their sons were to compete with these boys they would have to be well educated, too.

It was not merely this threat from the middle classes that brought about this change, however. The Renaissance had made people all over Europe much more interested in learning. Also the Reformation had stressed the need for people to think for themselves, and to do this everyone had to be as well educated as possible.

In later Tudor times some well-born boys were sent to the new grammar schools. But others, particularly if they lived in the country, continued their studies at home. Quite often they had a clergyman as a tutor, or, in Elizabethan days, one of the many well-educated Huguenots (Protestant refugees from France). Whether they went to school or not, the boys studied much the

same subjects. (We shall be looking more closely at the subjects taught in a grammar school in a later chapter.) The only difference was that the boys who were taught at home usually studied French and German, and perhaps even Italian, while modern languages were hardly ever taught in schools in the Tudor period.

Pastimes

As a relaxation, the boys learnt to play musical instruments. This was, in fact, thought to be an essential part of a noble-man's education all through the Tudor period. After dinner at night, noble families and their guests often entertained each other by playing and singing, and anyone who could not join in would have been considered very badly brought up.

The most popular instrument among the nobility for men and boys to play was the lute. This could be played either on its own or as an accompaniment to singing. But many boys of good family were also taught to play the harp. Henry VIII was very accomplished on the harp as a boy.

9　A page serves refreshments during an evening's musical entertainment in a wealthy household.

10　Young boys are playing with wooden knights on horseback, while others practise shooting with the longbow and crossbow.

Another popular instrument was the clavichord. It had a very simple keyboard, and was in fact, an elementary piano. For boys who were not musical there was an instrument called a viol-with-a-wheel. This looked something like a violin, but was played by turning a handle, like a small hurdy-gurdy.

The attitude to sport and games among the nobility was much the same as the attitude towards education. Boys were only permitted to play the kind of games which would be useful to them in adult life. For instance, they were nearly always taught to fence, in the hope that they would become good swordsmen, as noblemen in Tudor times frequently settled disputes with a duel. Similarly, the boys were usually taught jousting and tilting. Both of these gave them practice in fighting on horseback with a lance, which might have proved useful in battle. Even such sports as hunting and hawking were taught not so much for the boys' enjoyment as to prepare them to join the other members of the family in the field as soon as possible.

11 The lance shatters on impact as one knight tries to unhorse the other in a jousting tournament. The marshals ensure that the contestants obey the rules.

Family life

From the time they were quite small, boys in wealthy families ate their meals with the adults. This meant that they ate their main meal about eleven in the morning and their supper about five o'clock.

At the main meal, in particular, there was always a large choice of dishes, including some, like wild boar, peacocks, larks and seagulls, which are not eaten today. As it was difficult to keep food fresh, the meat and fish were always strongly seasoned. Cinnamon, cloves, vinegar and garlic were all used to try to disguise the fact that the food might have passed its best. Unless a salad was served at the beginning of the meal, there were no green vegetables. There might have been a few carrots or parsnips, but no potatoes as they were not grown in Britain in Tudor times.

The meat course was followed by various pastries and sweets, such as almond biscuits and marzipan. Then the meal ended with fruit (including imported fruit such as oranges and figs) and often some cheese. People usually drank ale, or perhaps wine with plenty of sugar in it (an Elizabethan had a very sweet tooth), although younger boys sometimes had barley water with spice in it instead.

Discipline was always rather strict in a Tudor household. As far as possible, no boyish pranks or mischief were ever allowed. Boys were made to work hard all the week and then go to church on Sundays. They also had to obey their fathers in everything, without question, or else they were soundly beaten.

Discipline had to be strict because families were so large in those days. It was not at all uncommon for a nobleman to have eleven or twelve children, or even more. Normally the household included also a number of aunts, uncles and cousins, as well as numerous servants, so that there might be

17

a vast number of people all living under one roof.

Boys were probably never made to wash behind their ears, however! Although young noblemen liked to wear perfume, very little attention was paid to cleanliness. Boys cleaned their teeth occasionally, with a piece of rag, and rinsed their hands. But to take off all your clothes and have a bath would have been thought positively dangerous!

12 Wealthy households were often quite large. The servants in the kitchen are plucking birds and roasting them on long spits in front of the fire.

3 Young Noblewomen

As babies, boys and girls were treated alike in noble families. They were all dressed in long, elaborately embroidered baby clothes with a tight-fitting embroidered cap. There were no special baby foods, so all small babies had to be fed by their mothers. But when they were a little older they had soft foods, like bread and milk, and sometimes a bone to gnaw to help them cut their teeth.

Both boys and girls must have liked nursery rhymes, just as they do today. All Tudor children knew 'Sing a Song of Sixpence', 'Three Blind Mice', 'Old King Cole', 'Ride a Cock Horse' and 'Ding Dong Bell'. In later Tudor times children also knew 'Mary, Mary, quite contrary'. Some people said that the Mary who was so contrary was really meant to be Queen Mary I.

There were no books specially written for children in Tudor times. But the grown-ups told the children the stories which they had heard when they were children themselves. Both boys and girls heard 'Tom Thumb', 'The Babes in the Wood', 'Jack the Giant Killer', 'Beauty and the Beast' and countless other stories which children still love today.

First lessons

Boys and girls were still treated the same when the time came for their first lessons. In wealthy families a tutor was engaged to teach the children as soon as they were two or three years old. This seems very young to us, but in the Tudor period people believed that children should learn to read and write almost as soon as they could say a few words.

Even rich children did not have a proper book for their first lessons. Instead they had a kind of wooden board, with a handle, which was known as a horn book. This looked like a modern chopping board, with a piece of paper stuck on one side, over which there was a very thin sheet of transparent horn to keep the paper clean. On the paper was written the alphabet, the numbers up to ten, and the Lord's prayer. The children would read these over and over again, sometimes saying, 'A for Apple, B for Ball', and so on, to help them remember the letters. Some very wealthy children also had building bricks with the letters on, so that they could spell out simple words, but they were not very common in Tudor times.

There were no lead pencils, or crayons of any kind, in those days. Also paper was far too expensive to be given to small children to write on. So even wealthy children first learnt to write on slates, or on special writing tablets, made of soft wax in a wooden frame, which could be used over and over again.

Children also learnt to count, with the aid of counting frames. They learnt their tables, as well, but normally only as far as the five times table. People in Tudor times had only recently changed from using Roman numerals to using Arabic ones, and even adults still found arithmetic rather confusing and difficult.

If children worked hard at their lessons they were often given a small reward. This

13 A wealthy mother dressed her child in long elegant dresses with lace ruffs, which restricted free movement and prevented participation in rough games. The sleeves of this infant's dress are exquisitely styled, and the bodice is decorated with braids and ribbons.

14 An Elizabethan horn book found during archaeological excavations at Brasenose College, Oxford. It includes the alphabet, pronunciation exercises, and the Lord's Prayer.

was usually a peppermint drop, or perhaps a small piece of gingerbread. Lazy children, on the other hand, were given a box on the ears, or even beaten, whether they were boys or girls, and even when they were little more than toddlers.

A girl's education

It was at about seven years old that a girl's life began to be different from her brother's. A boy was either sent away to be a page, or else he was sent to a grammar school; some girls from noble families also went as maids-in-waiting to other noble households, but there were no grammar schools that accepted girls in those days.

In fact, nearly all well-born girls were educated at home. Sometimes they were taught by a tutor or a governess, and sometimes by the family chaplain. As there were usually quite a number of children in every family, the class might be quite large, with the pupils varying in ages from seven to seventeen, or perhaps even older.

According to some writers, most of the tutors were overbearing and cruel. But there must have been some who were kind, like the tutor to Lady Jane Grey (1537-1554) — the tragic young girl who was Queen for nine days and then executed. In her own words, 'Master Elmer teaches me so gently, so pleasantly and with such fair allurements to learning' that she said the happiest hours of her life were the ones she spent in his company.

If a family were very rich they would often employ quite a number of tutors. One would teach the classics, one modern languages, one the sciences and so on. These tutors were often very scholarly men, who liked to live with a wealthy family, especially if the house had a fine library, so that they would have plenty of time and opportunity to pursue their own studies. As a result, well-born girls were often just as well educated as their brothers. This was true even in later Tudor times, when most wealthy boys went first to a grammar school

21

15   This finely dressed young lady is holding an astrolabe, which indicates that she was well educated. An astrolabe was an instrument used by navigators to calculate latitude, and by astronomers to gauge the altitude of the stars.

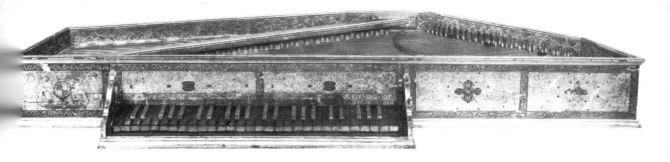

and then to a university. For example, modern languages had very little place in the grammar schools, and yet many well-born girls learnt to speak French and German fluently.

Music and dancing

Music was always part of a girl's education, as well. Every well-born girl was expected to be able to read a part in a song for four or five voices at sight, and also play several musical instruments. This was to enable her to join in the family entertainment when guests were invited to her home, or when she herself was a guest in someone else's house.

Girls, like boys, often played the lute and the flute. They also played the recorder (the same instrument that schoolchildren often learn to play today). Another very popular instrument among girls was the virginals. This was a keyboard instrument, in which the strings were plucked, instead of being hit by a hammer as in a piano.

Dancing was another important subject for girls. Every wealthy family held dances at Christmas, at weddings and on other festive occasions. In early Tudor times the dances usually took place in the dining hall, but by Queen Elizabeth's reign most stately homes had a long gallery where dances could be held.

One of the most popular dances with well-born young people was the galliard. This was a brisk, lively dance, mostly composed of a series of small running and leaping steps. In fact, it was rather like one of our present day folk dances, except

16 The virginal is a keyboard instrument in which the strings are plucked by quills. The keys are black instead of white, and the upper keys and wooden casing are delicately painted by hand.

that the male partners could introduce new steps of their own as they went along, if they wished.

There was not a great deal of opportunity for girls to take part in sport. In fact, unless they liked hunting and hawking, the only outdoor activity they could usually take part in was fishing. There were a few girls, however, who enjoyed archery, particularly in later Tudor times, when it had become merely a pleasant pastime, and was no longer a method of preparing for war.

Domestic arts

Girls in wealthy families usually learnt a great deal from their mothers. For instance, their mothers would teach them how to manage servants, and how to run a large household. In particular, they would show them how to budget household accounts, as this was always considered one of the duties of the wife in a rich Tudor family.

Mothers would also teach their daughters how to spin, to weave and to do fine needlework. (These were all thought to be essential accomplishments for every well-educated woman in Tudor times.) In addition, most mothers taught their daughters how to embroider. In Elizabethan times, in particular, English embroidery was considered to be the finest in Europe.

23

Well-born girls were not expected to bother with dull, everyday cooking. But their mothers would teach them how to prepare 'delicate dishes of their own devising', as one writer expressed it. This meant that they learnt how to distil rosewater, and other vegetable juices, to add colour and flavour to various dainty sweetmeats and preserves.

Mothers also taught their daughters how to prepare simple medicines for their families. These were mostly a mixture of the various herbs which Tudor people always grew specially for this purpose in their gardens. The cure for a headache, for

17 The cover of this book, said to have been worked by Queen Elizabeth, was embroidered in silver thread on black velvet. The book is 'Orationis Dominicae Explicatio', 1583

instance, was to drink the juice of lavender, bay, rue, roses, sage and marjoram, and for a bad chest a mixture of thyme, campanula and hyssop.

Miniature adults

Girls, like their brothers, were always dressed like miniature adults. In early Tudor times this meant that they wore long, loose-fitting gowns, with very wide, fur-edged sleeves. The fashionable neck-line was square, and cut low enough for the top of a brightly coloured undergown, or even a frilled chemise, to appear as an edging.

By the reign of Elizabeth, however, it had become the fashion to wear a farthingale. This was a series of hoops, made of cane, whalebone or wire, sewn into a petticoat to make the dress stand out. (Poorer girls made their dresses stand out much more cheeply, by tying a long roll of padding round their hips. This roll of padding was

known as a bum-roll.) Huge ruffs and large, padded shoulders also became popular among the rich, as did jewelled bodices, which came to a deep V at the waist in the front. Wealthy young women also liked to have an inverted V opening in the front of their skirts, from waist to hem, which would reveal a special underskirt made of some elaborate, contrasting material.

By the age of fifteen many well-born girls were married. (A girl was legally allowed to marry at twelve, and a boy at fourteen.) Romantic love usually had nothing to do with the marriage, though. It was merely arranged by the couple's parents in order to enlarge or improve their estates. In fact, some children were espoused while they were still quite tiny. This meant that the children were taken to church and they promised in front of the priest to marry as soon as they were old enough. This practice began to die out in later Tudor times, however, as people objected to parents 'forcing a marriage where there is no love, for the sake of material gain', as one writer expressed it.

18 'Woman and Four Children' by Hans Holbein II (1497-1543). The children wear the loose-fitting garments of the early Tudor period.

19 Children in the late Elizabethan period wore heavy dresses with farthingales, ruffs, padded sleeves and jewelled bodices ending in a low V shape. The boy in the centre wears a sash, a sword, and a pearl earring. Queen Elizabeth prided herself on having extremely dainty hands, and encouraged the mannerism displayed here of painting the hands as small and neat as possible.

Girls who did not marry had very little choice about the way they spent their lives. They could not go to the university, or train for one of the professions, like their brothers. In fact, before the Reformation it was generally taken for granted that any rich, unmarried girl would enter a convent, whether she felt any call to the religious life or not. After the Reformation an unmarried girl could not even become a nun. Indeed there was virtually nothing she could do but live at home with her parents, or with a married brother or sister. This meant that she usually had to occupy herself by spinning or weaving. It is for this reason that we still use the word 'spinster' (meaning someone who spins) for an unmarried woman even today.

20 The young princess Elizabeth in 1547, holding a gilt-edged book. Her costume is encrusted with jewels. Though she was often urged to form a matrimonial alliance, Elizabeth remained unmarried throughout her long reign.

4 Growing up in a Town

21 Westminster and Southwark, London, as they appeared in 1543. Most houses were built of wood, and fires were a frequent danger. Houses were also constructed on London Bridge, and sometimes they collapsed into the river. The north wall of the City of London is visible with its gatehouses leading out into open fields. Every small area had its own church, and the spires can be seen towering above the huddled houses.

In the Middle Ages there had been only two main social classes. One was made up of the landowners, who were very rich, and the other of the landless serfs, who were very poor. By the Tudor period, however, there was a new middle class. This was mostly made up of prosperous merchants and craftsmen, and a few professional men.

A merchant's son usually got up at about five o'clock (an hour later in winter). If he were lucky, a maid would bring him some hot water to wash with, and would lay out his clothes. When he was dressed he would go downstairs, and as soon as the rest of the family were ready, they would all say their morning prayers together, and then sit down to breakfast. In most Tudor families breakfast was just a few slices of bread and some home-brewed ale. There was sometimes a kind of porridge, though, made with peas or beans, or even some eggs, cheese or cold meat. The boy would not have much time to linger over the meal, however, as school began at six o'clock (an hour later in winter), and it might be quite a long walk to the school from his home.

22 A timbered Tudor house with the upper storey projecting over the lower one in order to gain more space. The overhanging houses made the streets very dark.

Home life: Before school

In Tudor times a well-to-do merchant usually lived in a large, comfortable house. It had to be large, because, in addition to the family, there were often half a dozen servants and several apprentices to be accommodated. In larger towns, the house was often just on the outskirts, facing the fields, and well away from most of the dirty, narrow streets, with their open sewers and piles of rubbish.

23 A four-poster bed, ornately carved, with embroidered curtains that could be closed for privacy.

A schoolboy sharpening his pen with his penknife. Behind him are examples of classical statues. Greek and Roman art, which had been rejected by medieval culture, was admired and revived by Renaissance artists and scholars. Tudor schoolchildren were taught to appreciate classical form and beauty.

Home life: After school

Before the Reformation a middle-class boy usually went to a Church school. In Elizabethan days, however, a middle-class boy would have gone to a grammar school. In either case, he would not have finished school until half past five in the evening (an hour earlier in the winter).

In the summer a schoolboy probably wandered home with his friends. He might even have stopped to kick a football about, or to have a game of leap-frog. In the winter, however, he would hurry home as quickly as possible. It was not safe to linger in the streets after dark, because there were so many thieves and vagabonds around. It was, in fact, very easy for a thief to creep up on someone unnoticed, for, apart from an occasional lantern hanging outside an inn or some large house, the streets were unlit. Rich people usually took a servant carrying a flare with them if they went out after dark, and the watch also carried flares, but a schoolboy just had to stumble along in the dark.

Before he left, he would have to pack his school satchel. For instance, he would need his ink-horn, filled with fresh ink, which was usually made at home. He would also need his quill pen, and his penknife for sharpening it. (This was the original use of the small knife we still call a penknife today.) In addition, he would usually have to take some writing paper. This cost fourpence a quire, and was much too expensive for the school to provide. Finally, in winter he would have to take some candles, as well, so that he could still see to do his lessons when it became dark in the afternoon.

When the boy reached home he would have a meal with the rest of the family. (He might have come home for a meal at midday, or he might have taken a packed lunch to school.) Grace was always said before meals in a middle-class Tudor household, and during the meal itself great importance was placed on good table manners among the children. There is, indeed, a book still in existence which was written to tell children how to behave. They were not to make faces or shout, or to take too big a mouthful of food or to gulp down their drinks too fast. They were not to play with their knives, shuffle their feet or blow on their food to try to cool it, and they were not to take all the best food for themselves but to share it with the rest of the family.

Pastimes

When the meal was over, the children might settle down to a game. They would probably know dozens of different forfeit games, guessing games and parlour games of all kinds. They might prefer to play a game with dice, however, or possibly draughts, chess or backgammon, which were all very popular in the Tudor period.

Children also liked cards, especially a game called 'Trump'. In this game all the players took turns in placing a card face upwards on the table. Then, whenever a certain card appeared, all the players had to hit the table with their left hands and shout, 'Trump!' Whoever was the last to hit the table and shout had to pay a small fine.

Children also amused themselves by asking each other riddles. A typical riddle was, 'Who killed a quarter of all the people

26   This sixteenth-century woodcut shows a popular street entertainer, Banks, with his performing horse 'Morocco'. The dice shown in the centre were often used in gambling games.

in the world?' (The answer was Cain, when he killed his brother, Abel.) Some of the riddles, especially the ones on religious subjects, were taught to the boys at school, as their teachers thought it was a good way of helping the boys to remember their lessons.

Children did not spend much time reading, as books were still very expensive. When they did have the chance to read, though, they often liked highly imaginative books, like *The Secrets and Wonders of the World* by the Roman writer Pliny. This contained strange stories of dogs that had hands and feet like men, and of fishes that came out of the sea at night, and ate all the corn in the farmers' fields.

Not even prosperous, middle-class people stayed up very late in Tudor times. The lighting in their houses was too poor, and in any case they had to be up very early in the morning. After family prayers, at which everyone, including the servants and the apprentices, had to be present, they usually went up to bed about nine o'clock.

25   The interior of a Tudor house had latticed windows, wooden wall-benches and heavy oak furniture. The fireplace was equipped with iron hooks and chains to hold cooking pots over the fire at various levels.

31

27 This engraving from John Day's 'Whole Book of Psalms', 1563, shows a Puritan family at prayer.

Saints days and holy days

Boys went to school six days a week in the Tudor period. Moreover, even on Sunday they could not do exactly as they liked, as they had to attend church at least once, and often twice. Before the Reformation, however, there were quite a number of saints' days and other holy days, when everyone, including boys at school, had a day off from work.

At Corpus Christi, in May or June, the festivities lasted for several days. As well as religious processions through the streets, most towns had one or more Mystery Plays, produced by the local trade guilds. Boys whose voices had not broken sometimes had the chance to take the female parts in these plays, as women were not allowed to perform in public in Tudor times.

Another exciting day for most schoolboys was December 6th. This was the Feast of St Nicholas (the original Santa Claus), who was the patron saint of children. On this day in nearly every large town a boy was chosen to be the 'boy bishop' for the year, and was given a bishop's mitre and cope. Then on December 28th, the Feast of the Holy Innocents, the 'boy bishop' and all his friends would take possession of the local cathedral, and conduct all the services (except Mass) for the day. This was a very popular event all through the Middle Ages, despite the fact that the Church did not altogether approve of it, and it was only abolished finally in the reign of Queen Elizabeth.

After the Reformation, most of the old religious feast days came to an end. But

28 This performance of a dramatic mystery play at Coventry shows a scene from 'The Life of Pontius Pilate'.

schoolboys still had a holiday on Shrove Tuesday, the last day before the long penitential season of Lent. They had pancakes, just as we do today, and even pancake races. But there was another strange custom on Shrove Tuesday in many schools at this period, as well. Each boy took the schoolmaster some money, with which he bought a fighting cock. The master then put a long string on the cock, and attached the other end to a post. Then all the boys took turns in trying to hit the cock by hurling a stick at it. If any boy succeeded, the cock became his, but if none managed to hit the cock then the schoolmaster kept it.

School holidays

There were no long school holidays in the Tudor period. Schools usually closed for sixteen days at Christmas and twelve days

29 The Globe Theatre on the south bank of the River Thames, where Shakespeare's plays were mainly performed.

About 1580 the first proper theatres began to be built. At first they were mostly on the south bank of the river in London, but before long they were being built in many other places as well. The stage itself was usually in the open air, although most of the audience was under cover, and the plays began about one or two o'clock in the afternoon, as there was no artificial lighting. When the theatres were first opened there was a great deal of rough, rowdy behaviour among the audience. For this reason most schoolboys, apprentices and university students were strictly forbidden to go to the theatre. There must always have been a few boys, though, who sneaked in with the rest of the crowd, and paid a penny or two to stand with the other laughing, shouting playgoers in the pit, as the cheapest part of the theatre was called in those days.

Girls

Turning to the girls in middle-class families, they were luckier than most girls in Tudor times. To begin with, they were often allowed to go to school with their brothers until they were seven years old. After that they had to stay at home with their mothers, but for a merchant's daughter there were always plenty of fairs and markets to pass the time, and often merchants from other interesting places to meet. When they were fifteen or sixteen years old some middle-class girls even became apprentices. They could learn such trades as embroidery or glove-making, and a few actually opened their own shops when they were older. This meant that, unlike most women in Tudor times, they were able to achieve a certain measure of independence, and choose for themselves the kind of lives they wanted to lead.

at Easter, but not at all in the summer. When a boy did have a holiday from school, however, there was always plenty for him to see and do, as towns were very lively, exciting places in Tudor times.

There was, for instance, nearly always a cock-fight he could watch. For a halfpenny he could perch on a wall surrounding the cock-pit, with all the other boys, for a whole afternoon. The cocks were not only specially trained to fight, but also had metal spurs attached to their feet, so that they could inflict as much damage as possible on each other, before one of them was finally torn to death. Alternatively, a boy could spend an afternoon watching bear-baiting or bull-baiting. In these so-called sports several fierce mastiffs would take it in turn to attack the huge, lumbering bear or bull. Although all these pastimes seem very cruel to us today, they were extremely popular with all classes of people in Tudor times, and a great deal of money was always wagered on the results.

If he were lucky, a boy might be able to watch a play. In early Tudor times there were no real theatres, but strolling actors often performed plays in the courtyard of an inn. The better-off people sat at the windows of the rooms overlooking the courtyard, but for a halfpenny a boy could stand in the courtyard itself and watch the performance.

5 Schools

'Better unborn than untaught'. This was a favourite saying in Tudor times among the ever increasing number of ambitious, middle class parents. By this they meant that it was essential for a boy to be well educated, if he were to succeed in life, particularly in an age when commercial activities were becoming more and more competitive every day.

Church schools

Before the Reformation education was mainly in the hands of the Church. The reason was that in the Middle Ages the clergy were often the only well-educated people in the community. Moreover, teaching was not looked upon so much as a job but as an act of charity, like helping the sick and needy, and so it was naturally regarded as the work of the priests.

From the age of five until they were seven boys usually went to a chantry school. (A chantry was a small chapel endowed by some rich person so that Mass could be said for the repose of his soul after he was dead.) The chantry's endowment often included some money for educational purposes, and as the chantry priest had no parish to look after he had plenty of time to give a few boys their first lessons.

From the age of seven until they were sixteen boys usually went to a choir school. These schools took their name from the fact that the boys were generally expected to sing in the church choir. Most of the choir schools were conducted by various orders of monks, in whatever time they had to spare from their usual work of running hospitals, almshouses, religious seminaries and so on.

There were only a handful of schools that did not belong to the Church in early Tudor times. There were a small number of 'petty schools', as they were called, and an even smaller number of grammar schools. The petty schools took boys (and sometimes girls) between the ages of four and seven, and were conducted by 'any poor women or others whose necessities compel them to undertake the task to save themselves from beggary', we are told. The grammar schools, on the other hand, only took boys between seven and seventeen years old. The teachers were usually well-educated men, who had been to the university. There was one important difference between the grammar schools and the choir schools, however. In the grammar schools the teachers were normally laymen, and not priests or monks.

The end of the Church schools

After the Reformation the Church schools were soon abolished. In the case of the chantry schools, this was not a very serious blow to education. They had only been teaching the very youngest children to read and write and to say their catechism, and they were quickly replaced in most places by new petty schools. The closure of the choir schools left a much more serious gap. Although Henry VIII said he would replace them with grammar schools, in fact less than twenty were founded during his reign. Under Edward VI and Mary only another forty or so were added, and by the time Queen Elizabeth came to the throne there were still far fewer schools of this type than there had been before the Reformation.

When Elizabeth became queen a new feeling of confidence swept the country. People felt certain that at last there would be a prolonged period of peace and prosperity. As a result, a large number of wealthy guilds and corporations, as well as a few private individuals, decided to devote some of their money to founding new grammar schools.

The new grammar schools

Within a few years there was a grammar school in almost every town. Some had only twenty or thirty pupils, and only needed one teacher and one assistant, or usher. But the average grammar school had at least one hundred boys, and some of the bigger, better known schools had between three hundred and four hundred pupils.

The majority of grammar schools in Elizabethan times were day schools. Indeed, the aim of the founders of most of the schools was to provide a place of education to meet local needs. A few of the larger schools had accommodation for boarders, however, and some of the others would find lodgings in the town for boys who came from a distance.

The Elizabethans believed that education should be free for everyone. But not all the grammar schools were well enough endowed to be able to teach all the boys for nothing. Some schools, for instance, only provided free education for 'natives' (that is for boys who lived in the immediate vicinity), and charged threepence or fourpence a week for teaching 'foreigners' (boys from other parts of the country). Other schools did not charge a weekly fee, but had an admission charge. This varied according to the parents' means, from ten shillings for a lord's son to fourpence for the son of a local burgess. In yet other schools most of the boys paid fees, but a few free scholars were accepted, if they would do odd jobs round the school, like lighting the fires and sweeping out the classrooms.

A schoolboy's day

School hours were long in the Tudor period. Boys were at school from six or seven o'clock in the morning to half past four or five in the afternoon. There was a two hour break for lunch, however, from eleven to one o'clock, when most of the boys went home, and two short breaks, at nine in the morning and three in the afternoon.

When a boy arrived at school he was expected to say 'good morning' to the master. Then he had to go straight to his place, and take out his books and writing materials quietly. (We know he had to do this, as there are still some 'Books of Manners' in existence, which were given to Elizabethan schoolboys to tell them how they were expected to behave.)

When it was time for school to begin, all the boys had to stand and say a prayer. They sometimes said a psalm, as well, or listened to a reading from the Bible. The school day always began and ended with this short act of worship, even after the Reformation, when there were few schools which still had any connection with the Church.

Once lessons began the boys knew that they would have to work hard all day. Nearly all the teaching was done by making the boys learn long passages from the textbooks by heart. This was not only thought to be the best method of teaching, but also meant that the boys' parents did not have to spend a great deal of money on buying books, which were extremely expensive in Tudor times.

If a boy did not learn all the work thoroughly he was thrashed. It never seems to have occurred to anyone that a boy might find the work difficult. He was just thought

30 This schoolroom in 1592 has many pupils. One teacher is beating a boy; the other teacher has discarded a broken whip behind his chair and is holding up another as the boys line up to recite their lessons.

to be lazy. If a boy fell too far behind, however, he was generally asked to leave the school, as there were always plenty of other boys only too anxious to take his place.

The syllabus

By far the most important subject on the school time-table was Latin. In fact, a grammar school originally meant a school in which Latin grammar was taught. The reason was not merely to give the boys a good classical education, but because Latin was of enormous practical value in Tudor times. If a person knew Latin he could make himself understood in any country in Europe. As a result, all commercial and political transactions with the Continent were conducted in Latin. Latin was also the language of the Church, of the law and of medicine. In fact, without Latin a boy had virtually no chance whatever of succeeding either in business or in the professions.

Latin was taught first by using it in everyday conversations. Indeed, by the time boys were nine or ten years old it was usually compulsory for them to speak Latin all day at school. Later the boys had to study Latin grammar thoroughly. They also had to read books written by the great Roman writers, like Virgil and Horace, to help them express themselves more fluently.

31 A letter written by Queen Elizabeth, on 1 January 1587, shows what Tudor handwriting looked like.

Some schools also taught Ancient Greek, and a few Hebrew. Modern languages, like French and German, were very rarely taught in a grammar school, however. English Literature was generally studied, especially in later Tudor times, but not for the purpose of teaching the boys to appreciate fine writing, so much as to help them improve their own style.

History rarely appeared on the time-table in a grammar school. There were also no regular Geography lessons, although some schools possessed a few maps and globes. The only form of Mathematics that was taught was Arithmetic, and this mainly consisted of learning to add up accounts, with the aid of counters and counting-frames.

Divinity took up a regular part of the school day, however. In most schools the boys had to learn the catechism, the new Protestant articles of faith and the Ten Commandments, all by heart. It was also the custom to test the boys every Monday morning on the sermon which they had heard in church the previous day, to make sure they had been attending!

Recreation

Music was very rarely taught in a grammar school in Tudor times. If it was, then it was usually regarded as an 'extra', for which the boys' parents had to pay. Although children of all classes knew how to play musical instruments, the study of the theory of music was considered of no great practical value, and was usually left to the nobility.

32 Musical notation looked slightly different from the way we write it today, but it is easily recognisable. This is one singer's part from a song for several voices designed to teach the alphabet.

The first part.

Cantus.

h, i, k, l, m, n, e, p, q, r, s & t, double w v, x, with y, ezod, & per se, con

fe, title title eft Amen. When you have done begin againe, begin againe.

Chriftes croffe be my fpeede in all vertue to proceede,

38

Towards the end of the Tudor period some schools began taking an interest in drama, however. This was no doubt due to the opening of the first purpose-built theatres, like 'The Globe'. The plays the boys performed were usually little more than a tableau, with some music and singing, but the boys must have found acting a pleasant change from their usual rather dull lessons.

There was no organized sport in schools in Tudor times. But in some schools one afternoon a week was set aside for some form of recreation. When the weather was bad, the boys usually spent the time playing draughts or chess, but in good weather they might go fishing or swimming, or perhaps practise archery.

Discipline was extremely strict in most of the grammar schools. Boys were thrashed even for such small faults as losing their caps or making fun of another boy. Most Tudor boys were quite accustomed to being thrashed at home, however, as Tudor parents would have thought they were failing in their duty if they had not beaten their children regularly.

Private schools

Towards the end of the Tudor period a new type of school appeared in some of the larger towns. This was a small, fee-paying school, run by some private individual for his own profit. These schools took boys of all ages, from five to seventeen, providing their parents were able to pay, and gave an education on rather similar lines to the grammar schools. The chief difference, however, was that the private schools taught modern languages. In fact, many of them were conducted by foreigners, particularly by Huguenot refugees from France. Some better-off merchants and professional men therefore thought it was worth paying the fees, as they believed that the ability to speak another modern language might be even more useful to their children than being able to speak Latin.

33 Swimming was a popular recreation for youths.

34 In this small classroom the children sit on benches, and have a large table on which they can place their inkwells, quill pens, penknives and compasses. In this more personal atmosphere, the teacher does not need to hold up a whip as a sign of authority.

6 Apprentices

The age at which a boy left school varied considerably in Tudor times. It might be as early as ten years old, or it might be as old as seventeen. Whatever the age, though, a boy could not begin earning his own living immediately he left school. He still had to receive some kind of further training, which in most cases meant that he had to become an apprentice.

This apprenticeship lasted by law for at least seven years. For some trades, and in some parts of the country, it was not unknown for it to last as long as ten. This meant that a young man might well be twenty-four years old or even older before he was 'free of his craft', as it was termed, and completely independent.

Choosing a craft

It would be impossible to list all the jobs for which a boy could become an apprentice. They varied from being a shearman, weaver, tailor or fuller to being a pewterer, or even an arrow-head maker. They also included such occupations as being a doctor or teacher, although in later Tudor times boys usually went to the university if they wanted to enter one of the professions.

A boy's first task was to find a master craftsman who needed an apprentice. By law a craftsman could only have two, or possibly three, apprentices for every journeyman he employed. This was to prevent the craftsman from using apprentices as cheap labour, and putting skilled journeymen, who had finished their apprenticeship, out of a job.

The next step was for the boy's father to pay the craftsman the necessary fees. This amount varied according to whether the craft was considered to be a high-class one, like a goldsmith's or a silversmith's, or not. Boys whose fathers did not possess at least forty shillings (or sixty shillings in the case of the high-class crafts) could not become apprentices in a town, but they were usually able to find apprenticeships in the country.

In return for this lump sum the master agreed to instruct the boy in his craft or trade. He also agreed to provide the apprentice with meat, drink, wearing apparel, lodgings and 'all other necessaries'. The master also promised to do his best to see that the apprentice worked hard, behaved himself during his leisure time and went to church at least once every Sunday.

The apprentice naturally had to make a number of promises on his part. For instance, he had to promise faithfully not to reveal any of his master's trade secrets, and to obey all his master's lawful commandments. He also had to promise 'not to absent himself from work either by day or by night unlawfully', not to gamble without his master's permission, not to go into taverns, and not to beg or to steal.

Terms and conditions

In early Tudor times it was the local guilds

35 A fifteenth-century woodcut of a boy apprentice carrying sheets of paper in a paper-making house.

which drew up these indentures. It was also the guilds who were responsible for seeing that the terms and conditions were kept. As there were separate local guilds for every craft and trade these conditions could vary considerably, not only from craft to craft but also very often from place to place.

In 1563 an important change took place,

36 These boy apprentices are working in an alchemist's laboratory. Alchemy was a science akin to chemistry, based upon the transmutation of metals. Alchemists believed that all metals were ultimately composed of one element, and by removing all the foreign matter (usually by fire) they could obtain, for example, pure gold from ordinary stones. They also sought a magical potion known as 'the elixir of life'.

37 The Court of Wards and Liveries (about 1588). This body organized trade and industry under the control of guilds or companies of privileged tradesmen and craftsmen. The twelve Great Companies were (and still are today) the Mercers, Grocers, Drapers, Fishmongers, Goldsmiths, Skinners, Merchant Tailors, Haberdashers, Salters, Ironmongers, Vintners and Clothworkers.

however. An act was passed, called the Statute of Artificers, which brought apprentices directly under the control of the government. The aim was to ensure as far as possible that all apprentices, whatever their craft and wherever they worked, were bound by exactly the same terms and conditions.

Under this act the wages an apprentice received were laid down by the government.

Hours and conditions of work were also controlled on a national basis. Even the clothing that an apprentice was allowed to wear, and the type of amusement that he could take part in, were all laid down in considerable detail in the act.

Even after the act, life was still not the same for all apprentices, however. In fact, whether they had a happy, profitable apprenticeship or not still depended almost

entirely on their master. There were some masters, for instance, who taught their apprentices little or nothing of value about their craft, and even made them sleep on the floor under the workbench, or under the shop counter. On the other hand, there were some masters who treated their apprentices like their own children. In this case, the apprentices often learnt a great deal more than merely how to be a competent craftsman. These kindly masters sometimes took their apprentices into partnership with them when the boys grew up, and they sometimes even left a particularly favoured apprentice their business when they died.

43

38   A tailor's shop. A lady's farthingale hangs on
the wall, and the dress will be shaped round the
hoops. The apprentices themselves wear plain, sober
clothes in accordance with the laws.

Behaviour

Throughout the whole Tudor period apprentices were notorious for their bad behaviour. They were continually quarrelling amongst themselves, and were frequently involved in drunken brawls. In fact, strangers to a town were often terrified of meeting a gang of apprentices, as they knew that many of them considered it a great game to hurl stones or bricks at a 'foreigner'.

It was quite usual for apprentices to form themselves into gangs. They would then roam the streets after work looking for a rival gang they could fight. As soon as they saw one a shout of 'Clubs!' would go up, and they would pull out their cudgels and do their best to break open their rivals' heads. The butchers' apprentices would fight the weavers', the bakers' would fight the masons', the carpenters' the potters', and so it would go on. Usually no great harm was done, apart from a few broken noses, but sometimes an apprentice might have a sword (although this was strictly forbidden), and do his opponents some serious injury.

Easter, May Day and Whitsun were the worst times for these fights. The apprentices usually had several days holiday, and they would spend almost the entire time either drinking or brawling. In fact, it was not unknown for the authorities to order a curfew during the holiday period, which meant that all apprentices had to be indoors from nine in the evening until seven the following morning.

An apprentice who was caught misbehaving was usually fined on the first occasion. If he was caught again, however, he was taken to the guild hall and whipped before all his fellow apprentices. It never seems to have occurred to anyone that what was really needed was more opportunity for the apprentices to work off their natural high spirits and energy in some kind of sport or other recreation.

Wealthy boys: Dress

In later Tudor times the authorities were faced with a new problem. This was due to the ever increasing number of boys from upper class families who were becoming apprentices. Just as the gentry were at last realizing the importance of giving their sons a sound academic education, so they were also becoming increasingly aware of the need to have their sons taught a trade.

As might be expected, the problem was worst in the City of London. In fact, there were soon so many apprentices there whose fathers were 'persons of quality' that special measures were needed to deal with them. One of the main difficulties was that these boys were naturally used to wearing 'costly apparel'. Indeed, their clothes were often much more expensive and elegant than those of their masters.

As a result a special order was issued in 1582 by the Lord Mayor. This repeated the previous regulations about dress, and tried to insist on uniformity. It said that no apprentice was allowed to wear 'great breeches with stuffing' or padded jackets. Instead he had to wear a 'small, plain slop, made of fustian, leather or wool', with no ruffs or embroidery. An apprentice was not even allowed to dress in the fashionable colours — peach, orange or flame. Everything he wore had to be either a dull blue, russet, white, fawn or grey. Apprentices were also forbidden to wear their hair long, in any of the fashionable styles, and in particular they were not allowed to have 'locks of hair around their ears'.

For most apprentices, though, the most irksome rule concerned their headgear. According to the new order, every time they stepped out into the street they had to wear a plain, flat, woollen cap. This was not only unfashionable, but marked them out as apprentices, instead of the fashionable young men about town which they would have liked to have appeared.

39   Inspectors check the weights and measures of
shop traders. Dishonest shopkeepers who gave short
measures were often punished in public.

Wealthy boys: Amusements

Boys from upper class families also posed problems when it came to their leisure time. The only pastimes that most apprentices took part in were running races, wrestling and swimming. There were a certain number, however, who took part in archery or pole-fighting (fighting with a long stick, which had to be tightly grasped with both hands all the time).

Boys from wealthy families, on the other hand, liked dancing and going to the theatre. Neither of these were considered suitable occupations for apprentices, and were usually forbidden. Worse still, many of them enjoyed fencing, which was not only considered unsuitable, but also likely to lead to serious injuries if the boys carried swords and became involved in a fight.

We know that some apprentices managed to get round these restrictions, however. They would keep a secret supply of fashionable clothes at a friend's house, and change into them as soon as their work was finished. They would then go dancing or fencing or to the theatre, and hope that no one would recognize them as apprentices, and report them to their masters.

An apprentice's day

The work done by an apprentice naturally varied according to his craft. When he first became an apprentice he probably spent most of his time running errands and sweeping out the workshop. If his master was a shopkeeper, however, as well as a craftsman (which was quite usual in Tudor times), an apprentice often looked after the shop while the master and his journeymen worked in a back room.

In this case, the apprentice's day would begin by taking down the shop's shutters. He would then sweep any rubbish into the street, and set out the goods to be sold on the shop counter. After that the apprentice would take up his place at the shop doorway, and try to persuade passers-by to come in and buy, by shouting, 'What do ye lack? What do ye lack? Come and buy!'

If he were lucky, the apprentice would sometimes have some more interesting jobs to do. For instance, he might go to the market, and help his master buy some of the materials he needed for his work. If he lived in London, he might even go to the wharves, where ships unloaded goods from abroad, and help his master select what he needed, and then carry it home.

As time went on, the apprentice was allowed to do more and more of the actual work of his craft. He would probably begin by holding the tools for his master, and watching him work. Then he would be allowed to do some of the very simplest jobs for himself. But a master always took care to see that an apprentice did not learn all the trade secrets before his apprenticeship was finished!

40 This silver Tudor standing dish (bearing a London hallmark for 1564-5) is an example of the fine craftsmanship expected of an apprentice after his long training.

7 The Universities

In Tudor times most boys became apprentices when they left school. But a few, who were more interested in learning than the others, went to the university instead. There were only two universities in this country at that period. One was Oxford, which had about sixteen hundred students, and the other was Cambridge, which was not quite so large.

41   A class in a sixteenth-century university.

The students

In early Tudor times nearly all the students were clerks. This meant that they intended to enter the Church, and were receiving their education for nothing. Nearly all of them came from the middle or lower classes. The only boys from rich families were those who were too weak or sickly to live an active, outdoor life.

The age at which a boy went to the university varied considerably. In the case of a nobleman's son, it was not unknown for it to be as young as ten or eleven years old. The average age, however, in early Tudor times was about fifteen, and by Queen Elizabeth's reign the average had risen to about seventeen years old.

There were several colleges at each university even in early Tudor times. But most of the colleges only had living accommodation for the fellows and the senior students. A few of the undergraduates lived in hostels, but most of them had to find their own accommodation, either in cheap lodging houses in the town or in inns.

This made it difficult for the authorities to keep a proper eye on the students. So, not surprisingly, the students had the same sort of reputation for rowdy behaviour as the apprentices. There were constant complaints from the townspeople about fighting and drunkenness, and about noisy, unruly behaviour in general.

There was certainly a great deal of horse-play among the students. We know, for example, that when a boy first went to the university he was often set upon by

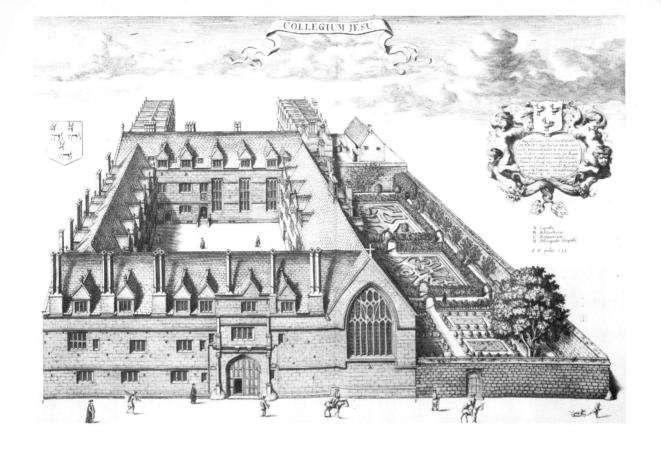

COLLEGIUM JESU

some of the older students, and ordered to tell them some jokes. If the jokes amused them they would give him a tankard of beer. If not, they would seize him and force him to drink salt and water until he was sick.

The Reformation

During the Reformation the number of students at the universities fell sharply. There was so much disturbance at both Oxford and Cambridge that parents were unwilling to take the risk of sending their sons there. The fellows and senior students were constantly being arrested, and whole libraries of books had to be destroyed because they were unacceptable to the government of the day.

The universities remained in this sorry state for several years. But with the accession of Queen Elizabeth they quickly began to flourish again. There were many new schools

42   Jesus College, Oxford

where boys could be prepared for the university, and, more important still, people were beginning to feel confident that the troubled times were over at last.

After the Reformation there were far more wealthy boys at the universities. As we saw in earlier chapters, upper class families were at last beginning to realize the importance of study. The admission of these rich, fee-paying students caused a certain amount of resentment, however, as both Oxford and Cambridge had originally been founded for the education of 'poor scholars'.

Unfortunately, some of these better-off students did not take their studies seriously. They brought the universities 'into much slander', one writer tells us, because of their gaudy clothes and riotous behaviour. 'And for excuse', he adds tartly, 'when they are charged with breach of all good order, they think it sufficient to say in their defence that they are gentlemen'.

There had been constant complaints about the students' behaviour before the Reformation, of course. But by Elizabethan times they were all living in college, and the behaviour of most of them had obviously improved. So it is not surprising that the authorities should have been concerned about the new fee-paying students, and should have drawn up a number of strict new regulations.

Rules and regulations

The new regulations for the students were similar to the rules for apprentices. At Oxford, for instance, no student was allowed to go into taverns, or into any shops where tobacco was sold. They were also forbidden to go to the theatre, or to play football. The punishment in every case, if they were caught, was to be publicly whipped.

At Cambridge a student was fined if he did not wear 'a gown reaching to the ankles'. He was also fined for wearing silks or satins, 'excessive ruffs', or 'stockings of unseemly greatness'. In addition, both universities fined students who did not attend church on Sundays. They were expected to attend both at five o'clock in the morning and again in the evening.

Some individual colleges also laid down rules for their students. One college, for example, fined any student who was seen with 'an inordinate length of hair'. Another birched any student who 'prevented his fellows from studying or sleeping by singing, making a noise, shouting, or discharging guns, or by making any other kind of uproar or din'.

Wealthy students

Life was pleasanter for the students once they were able to live in college. (Life did, in fact, become more comfortable for almost everyone in the latter part of the Tudor period.) Nevertheless, boys from wealthy families still had a much higher standard of living at the university than the poorer students, and this was yet another reason why they were generally disliked.

A nobleman's son, for instance, would have a warm, comfortable room to himself.

43 Wealthy young men preferred to wear the fashionable large ruffs, colourful silks and satins, short cloaks, and fine stockings of the man-about-town. Students were not allowed to indulge in such finery.

It would be furnished with a feather bed, a chest for his clothes and another chest for his linen. There would probably be expensive velvet curtains at the windows, and the student could have clean rushes strewn on the floor as often as he wished.

A poor student, on the other hand, would have to share a room. In fact, it was quite common for two or three poor students to have to sleep in the same bed. There was no fire, unless the students gathered some sticks for themselves, and the furniture would probably just consist of a rough trestle table and some benches.

Even the food varied according to the students' means. (The colleges provided dinner and supper, but the students had to provide their own breakfast.) In the college dining-room all the choicest dishes were on the top table, which was only for the fellows and the very wealthiest fee-paying students. The next table had quite appetizing, but much plainer, food. This was for the other graduates, and for ordinary, middle-class fee-paying students. It was at the third table, however, that the students of 'low condition' sat, and they usually had little more than some soup and bread, some boiled beef, and a halfpenny worth of beer each.

In fact, the food for the poorer students was barely enough to keep them alive. So they were always looking for ways of making a little money to buy themselves a few extras. One way they could earn money was by doing odd jobs for the richer students, like waking them up in the morning, cleaning their shoes and running on little errands for them.

The syllabus
It took four years to become a BA, and a further three to become an MA. The syllabus for both degrees was the same, although the subjects were naturally studied at more depth for the MA. In each case the subjects were Grammar, Logic and Rhetoric (these were known as the Trivium), and Arithmetic, Geometry, Music and Astronomy (known as the Quadrivium).

This syllabus was much the same as the one the students had followed in the Middle Ages. What was more, it remained basically the same throughout the whole of the Tudor period. The method of instruction had not changed appreciably since the Middle Ages, either. The only person who normally had a book was the lecturer, just as in the days before printing was invented.

Debates were also just as important as in the Middle Ages. Students would still spend hours discussing such points as 'How many angels could sit on the point of a pin?' This was supposed to teach them to think logically and to express themselves clearly, so that the people who were listening could follow their arguments. Even the examinations took the form of debates. To obtain a BA, for instance, a student had to take part in four 'disputations', as they were called, in front of their college fellows. One student proposed a motion while another opposed it. These disputations lasted from one o'clock in the afternoon until five, with an hour's break about three o'clock for refreshments.

Later Tudor times
In later Tudor times the authorities became much stricter about study. For example, any students who failed to attend their lectures regularly were fined. Also examinations were much more carefully supervized, and the old practice of allowing rich students to purchase degrees, to which they were not really entitled, was abolished.

There were still no tutorials as we know them today. But as more and more wealthy students joined the universities, it became quite common for their parents to engage private tutors for them. If a student were very wealthy he might have his own personal tutor, but it was more usual for five or six students to have one tutor between them, and for their parents to share the expense.

After the Reformation all students had to acknowledge the reigning monarch as the Head of the Church. They also had to accept the Thirty-Nine Articles of the Protestant faith, and the Protestant prayer-book. At first this did not appear to make a great deal of difference. But after the laws were tightened in 1570 any Catholics who wanted a university education were forced to go abroad.

44 An engraving of William Shakespeare (1564-1616) by Martin Droeshout, which was prefixed to the first folio edition of his plays in 1623.

The Inns of Court
When they left the university, some students went to one of the four great Inns of Court, in London. (In fact, quite a number of noblemen's sons went there straight from school, instead of going to Oxford or Cambridge.) These Inns of Court only taught legal subjects, but they had such a high reputation that they were described by one writer of the period as England's 'third university'.

The Inns of Court laid great stress on cultural and social activities. For example, while students at Oxford and Cambridge were forbidden to visit the theatre, the Inns of Court were actively encouraging drama. Indeed, two plays by William Shakespeare (1564-1616), *Twelfth Night* and *The Comedy of Errors*, were both given what is thought to have been their first performances, not in a theatre, but in one of the Inns of Court.

8 Growing up in the Country

The middle class people in the country were the yeomen. The term 'yeoman' had originally meant someone who was not of noble birth but who owned his own land. By Tudor times, however, any prosperous farmer was described as a yeoman, regardless of whether his land was freehold or was rented from the lord of the manor.

45   This sixteenth-century woodcut of a country scene shows two children standing in front of a well. Men and women slaughter animals for winter meat, and in the background they gather fruit and chop wood for winter fuel. The windmill in the distance was used to grind the corn to flour. From an upper storey window dirty water is being emptied into the courtyard. Insanitary practices such as these gave rise to unhealthy living conditions.

Yeomen in Tudor times

One writer of the time tells us that his father was a yeoman. He says that his father owned no land of his own, but rented enough to keep six farm-workers busy. His father also had thirty cows, which his wife helped him to milk, as well as a flock of one hundred sheep, which he kept mainly for their wool.

In some ways a prosperous yeoman was better off than a member of the gentry. His income was often just as great, but he was content to live much more frugally. He did not have to spend money on a grand house, or on lavish entertaining, or even on assisting the needy, but could use most of his profits for improving his land. In fact, by diligence, thrift and foresight many yeomen attained considerable wealth. They were then sometimes able to buy some of the land that belonged to some unthrifty nobleman. If their sons were also astute and hard working they might manage to increase the size of their estate until eventually the family were rich enough to call themselves gentlemen.

Babies

There was always great rejoicing when a baby was born in a yeoman's family. All the friends and neighbours brought presents, and drank the baby's health in ale or wine. A special cake was baked, and there was music and dancing. In fact, a wealthy

46   A map of Whatborough manor in Leicestershire, 1576, shows how the small 'townes' were linked by narrow country roads. The abbey on the right has extensive grounds to grow its own food. The fields were divided up into strips in the medieval way, so that each yeoman had small manageable fields in both good and bad farming land. This map quotes the method of measurement as being 'sixteene foote and an halfe to the pearche'.

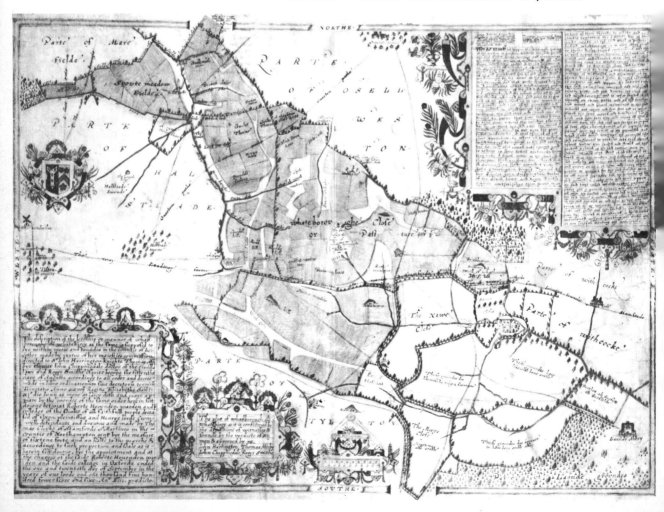

yeoman might even light a bonfire outside his house, like the gentry did when a baby was born.

For country people there were a great many superstitions surrounding a birth. For instance, the church bells in the nearest village always had to be rung while the baby was being born. The bells were believed to frighten away any wicked spirits that might be flying around, and prevent them from casting a spell on the child.

Another country belief was that the fairies sometimes stole a child, and left in its place an ugly, mischievous fairy child, called a changeling. The only way of protecting the baby was to have it baptized as quickly as possible. (Babies were usually baptized on the day they were born, in any case, as a great many children died in infancy in Tudor times.)

It was also considered very unlucky to dress a new born baby in new clothes. So, for the first few hours of its life, a baby born in the country was always wrapped in a piece of old cloth. Then the cloth would be taken off, and the baby would be wrapped in swaddling clothes for a month or two (like all Tudor babies), before being dressed in its first proper baby clothes.

Country people always looked at the stars when a baby was born. They thought that the position of the various planets would tell them what kind of life the baby would have in the years to come. If the stars foretold that the baby would have a happy, prosperous life this was, of course, the signal for even more rejoicing and merrymaking.

Schooldays

When the children were three or four years old it was time for their first lessons. Usually both boys and girls were taught to read and write by the parish priest or the parish clerk. Then, at the age of seven, the boys were sent to the nearest school, for the average yeoman was just as anxious as the middle-class people in the towns for his sons to be well educated.

When he was older the yeoman's son might become an apprentice, or even go to the university. But much more often he stayed at home, and helped his father on the farm. Farming was one of the few occupations for which it was not possible to become an apprentice, as even the smallest estates normally remained in the hands of the same family for generations.

47 Boys worked with their fathers on the land, helping to plough the fields with horses or oxen, and sowing or setting the seed into the tilled soil.

Much of a country boy's spare time was usually spent with the county militia. As there was no regular, standing army in Tudor times, this part-time force was the nation's front line of defence. In fact, in early Tudor times boys were forbidden to play football, or any other 'unlawful games', in case they spent too much time amusing themselves, when they should have been practising at the butts.

Practically every village had its own branch of the militia. As one writer tells us, 'There is almost no village, be it never so small, that hath not sufficient arms in readiness to send forth three or four men'. He then adds that 'the amour and munition is kept in one certain place, appointed by the consent of the whole parish, where it is always ready to be had and to be worn within the hour'.

A typical village could provide one archer, one gunner, one pikeman and one billman (a bill was a kind of curved battle-axe, with a long wooden handle). In early Tudor times the archer was easily the most important member of any fighting force, but during the course of the sixteenth century bows were gradually discarded in favour of fire-arms.

48   Practising at the butts with a crossbow.

49   A nobleman wore armour in battle, and the sword was his main weapon. The footsoldier of 1590 wore a metal helmet and breastplate, and carried firearms. The horn slung from his neck held the gunpowder for his arquebus and pistol.

Girls

While the boys were at school, the girls were taught at home by their mothers. They did not spend much time on books, but concentrated mainly on such things as spinning and weaving. Indeed, a country girl's education was not considered complete until she had made a full set of bed linen and table linen (for her bottom drawer), as well as a complete set of clothes.

The girls were also taught how to prepare the family's meals. In early Tudor times the staple foods in a yeoman's household were brown bread, cheese and eggs, with occasionally some chicken or pork. By Elizabethan times, however, the better-off families had a much more varied and interesting diet. In fact, they often ate almost as much of the expensive foods, like beef and mutton, as the nobility did.

Another skill that girls had to learn was how to look after the dairy. Milking the cows and caring for the calves was always regarded as a woman's job in the Tudor period. In fact, there were countless tasks, from baking bread and brewing beer to making candles, that every yeoman's daughter had to learn before she was considered capable of running a home of her own.

Country festivals

Although country people had to work hard, they probably had the happiest lives in Tudor times. In fact, it is of the yeomen that people are usually thinking when they refer to Tudor times as the days of 'Merrie England'. Every season seemed to bring a new reason for merrymaking, and the yeoman's family usually had the time and the money to enjoy all these occasions to the full.

In early Tudor times many of these festivities were connected with saints' days and holy days, and even after the Reformation several of these old religious festivals survived. Shrove Tuesday, for instance, the last day before the long, penitential season of Lent, was always a time of great fun and merrymaking all through the Tudor period.

In most villages there were games of tossing the pancake. And in some villages there were races, with all the competitors tossing their pancakes as they ran. There was usually cock-fighting, as well, although this was a very cruel sport, as the cocks had sharp pointed spurs attached to their claws, and often tore each other to death.

Another traditional amusement on Shrove Tuesday was a kind of riotous football game. All the young people of one village would challenge the youths of a neighbouring village to a match. The two villages themselves were the goals, and so the ball often had to be kicked or carried for several miles. It was 'verily a game both rude and rough', one writer informs us.

May Day was another time of great merriment for country children. Very early in the morning all the young people of the village would go into the neighbouring woods to gather flowers and leafy branches. Then they would cut down a tall, straight tree to be their maypole, and it would be dragged into the village by a team of oxen, and set up on the village green. Once it was firmly in position, each boy and girl would take hold of one of the ribbons tied to the top, and the traditional May Day dancing would

50 May Day celebrations in the town. Permanent maypoles were set up in London, but were later destroyed by Puritans in the seventeenth century. This was the maypole before St Andrew Undershaft. A friar and a jester are dancing with the townspeople while a May Queen presides over the festivities.

begin. These May Day festivities had their origins far back in pagan times, and were supposed to ensure that the cows gave plenty of milk and that there would be a good harvest.

The next great festival for country people took place at harvest time. The last sheaf of corn to be cut was dressed up as a girl, and was called the 'Harvest Queen'. Then, after a harvest thanksgiving service in the village church, the 'Queen' was taken into a large barn, where everyone had a special harvest supper of roast goose and home-brewed ale.

Only a few weeks later there was the exciting festival of Hallowe'en. Like May Day, this had originally been a pagan festival, and had only later become associated with All Saints' Day. Bonfires were lit to scare off witches, or any other wicked spirits, and the children made masks and lanterns, and played traditional Hallowe'en games, like ducking for apples.

Christmas time

Christmas was the longest holiday in the year for country people. It began on Christmas Eve, when every village and hamlet chose its own 'Lord of Misrule'. He and his friends then dressed up rather like Morris men, with bells tied on their legs, and went dancing and singing up and down all the lanes.

On Christmas Day itself everyone naturally had a great feast. People also gave each other presents, although the present giving sometimes did not take place until New Year's Day. The presents were very much the same as we give today — handkerchiefs, gloves, cushion covers, brooches, bracelets, inkhorns, and, of course, toys and sweets for the children.

On Twelfth Night every family had a huge cake with a silver coin hidden in it, and whoever found the coin in his slice of cake became the 'King' for the day. Also on Twelfth Night all the children in the country districts went wassailing, and sang Christmas songs and carols outside their neighbours' houses for cakes, sweets or small gifts of money.

Devils and other wicked spirits were supposed to be about on Twelfth Night. So all the country people chalked crosses on the beams inside their houses to try to protect themselves. They did not go back to work directly after Twelfth Night, however, like the townspeople, but went on enjoying themselves until 'Plough Monday', when the long Christmas holiday at last came to an end.

9 Poor Children

We mentioned in an earlier chapter that the Tudor period was a time of great change, and nowhere is this more clearly to be seen then in the case of the poor. At the beginning of the Tudor age there were still many thousands of poor people living reasonably happy, secure lives in the country, just as they had done all through the Middle Ages. By the end of the Tudor period, however, their numbers had fallen dramatically. Those who were still living in the country probably had a slightly higher standard of living than they would have had in earlier times. But the great majority of these poor people had left the country, and turned themselves into a vast new army of beggars and vagrants in the towns.

Early Tudor times

Let us begin by looking at the poor as they were in very early Tudor times. Most of

them were farm-workers — ploughmen, cowmen, shepherds, swineherds and the like. There were a certain number, however, who were village artisans — cobblers, weavers, blacksmiths, bricklayers, carpenters and so on.

Whatever their job, they never possessed any land of their own. They just lived and worked on the estates of the local lord of the manor. They were nearly always allowed to keep a few cows and pigs, though, on the common land around the village, so they were to some extent self-supporting.

The homes of these poor people were naturally rather primitive. They usually lived in a one-roomed thatched cottage, or perhaps just a turf-covered hut. There was no chimney, so the cottage was constantly full of smoke, and little artificial lighting beside a few home-made candles or rush-lights. The floor was just made of hard earth, which it was impossible to keep clean. And as all the water had to be brought from a well, very little washing could have been done. Nevertheless, these poor people probably thought they had all they needed — a trestle table, a few stools and perhaps a chest in which to store their few humble possessions.

On the whole these poor country people ate reasonably well. In a good year they

51 Women and children of poor families worked in the fields. Girls would wear calf length skirts, as the more fashionable long dresses were impractical for work. The young woman carrying hay on the left is too poor to buy shoes.

had plenty of milk, eggs and cheese, and sometimes even some meat from their own livestock. It was only when the harvest was bad that they had to make do with 'horse-corn' (a rough, dark bread made from peas, beans and oats) and whatever berries and nuts they could find.

Country children

Most country children began helping their parents almost as soon as they could walk. At the age of five or six, for instance, they were often sent to look after the animals that were grazing on the common land. Or they might be sent into the fields when the seeds had just been sown, to scare the birds away by hurling stones at them from their catapults.

When they were older the boys were often sent into the woods to collect firewood. In the autumn they might also collect acorns and beech-nuts as food for the pigs. When they were older still they would generally help with the ploughing, and might even do such heavy, back-breaking work as pruning, hedging or ditching.

The girls in these poor families often worked just as hard as the boys. As well as doing their share of the work in the fields, they also had to assist their mothers in the home. At a very young age they began helping their mothers spin and weave clothes for the family, in addition to doing quite an amount of the washing and cooking.

Another job that was often done by the girls was to collect the rushes from the river, and then peel them and dip them in wax, in order to make the rush lights for their cottages. It was usually the girls' job, too, to look after the bees. Sugar was very expensive in Tudor times, and for most people the only form of sweetening was honey.

Most of these poor country children received little or no education. If they were lucky they might be taught the rudiments of reading and writing by the parish priest or the parish clerk. But, except for a few very intelligent boys who were chosen to go to school to train as priests, most of them were fortunate if they were even able to write their names when they grew up.

The demand for wool

Many of these poor country families had been working for the same landowners for generations. And no doubt most of them thought that their way of life would continue in much the same way for ever. But, in fact, a dramatic change had already begun to take place long before the first of the Tudors came to the throne, although the full effects were not to be felt until the reign of Queen Elizabeth.

The change had, indeed, begun in the early part of the fourteenth century, and was due to an enormous new demand among the weavers on the Continent for English wool. The demand was so great that the English landowners had soon realized that they could make far more money by keeping sheep than by continuing to grow crops on their land. This in turn had led to ever increasing unemployment among the farm-workers, as it required only one man to look after a flock of sheep where six had been employed tilling the soil. To make matters worse, most of the common land was gradually being fenced in by the rich landowners, and this meant

that the poor could not even make ends meet by keeping a few cows or pigs.

There seemed nothing these poor people could do but leave their homes, and the villages where they had been born and brought up, and to try to find some kind of work somewhere else. Wherever they went, though, they found the situation much the same, and the vast majority of them ended up as vagrants, wandering from one place to another, either begging or stealing.

53   Sir Thomas More and his family in 1593.

'What else can they do', asked Sir Thomas More (1478-1535, Lord Chancellor under Henry VIII and a great philosopher and writer) 'but steal, and then be hanged, or else go about begging? Poor, simple, wretched souls — men, women, husbands, wives, fatherless children, widows, woeful mothers and their young babes — they have to trudge on and on.'

Beggars and vagabonds

It has been estimated that by Tudor times there were as many as ten thousand of these vagrants. Most of them were in London

54   Beggars coming into town. The children in the panniers may be the offspring of beggars, or they may be abandoned children whom the vagrants have found or brought to help them with their begging. In the background a line of destitute people queue up for the parish poor relief.

and the other large towns, like Bristol, Norwich and Lincoln. Even the smaller towns had their share of these wretched people, who were continually moving from one place to another in a desperate attempt to find a home and some work.

The genuinely destitute were not the only vagrants in Tudor times, though. There were, in addition, a certain number of others who preferred to beg and steal rather than to do an honest day's work. These rogues and vagabonds just took advantage of the fact that the country was swarming with beggars in order to trick, or even terrorize, simple, unsuspecting people into giving them alms.

Before the Reformation the authorities were not too concerned about the vagrants. They knew that every town had its monasteries and nunneries where the poor could get a meal and sometimes even a bed. But after the dissolution of the monasteries there was no one to whom these poor people could turn, and, to make matters worse, their numbers were increasing all the time at an alarming rate.

In fact, the position was soon so bad that the local authorities could no longer ignore it. But instead of considering ways of helping the needy, they usually just took the view that it was a person's own fault if he were poor. Indeed, they generally whipped anyone they found begging, or put him in the stocks, in order to teach him not to be lazy and idle, and then sent him back to the parish from which he had come.

Homeless children

As is usually the case, it was the children who suffered most in this situation. Indeed, most of the children born into these poor, vagrant families were lucky if they even managed to survive. The death rate among children under five of all classes in Tudor times was eight out of nine, but among the poor the proportion must have been very much higher.

The chief cause of death among these poor, homeless children was malnutrition. But in many other cases children were just left to die because their parents had no means of looking after them. In some old churches today you can still see parish registers with entries recording the burial of children found dead in the streets from exposure and starvation, because their parents had abandoned them.

The children of rogues and vagabonds were probably fortunate if they did not live. If they did, they were usually forced into a miserable, humiliating life of begging and stealing from a very early age. Worse still, it was not at all uncommon for these wretched children to be deliberately crippled

55 Orphans of the rich were luckier than the poor, since they were readily adopted by guardians eager to manage their estates until they came of age. Money was an important consideration in such transactions, as the man on the left with his hand in his money-pouch shows.

by their parents, so that people would take pity on them, and give their rascally parents some alms.

Concern for poor children

Right from the beginning of Tudor times there was a certain amount of concern over poor children. Indeed, almost as soon as the monasteries were dissolved the first act was passed to try to protect them. This instructed parish councils to find apprenticeships for any healthy children, between the ages of five and fourteen, who were found begging or wandering about the streets apparently destitute.

Unfortunately, this act did not work as well as had been hoped, for the simple reason that there were not many craftsmen who were willing to take dirty, illiterate urchins as apprentices. In fact, it was usually only the very poorest types of craftsmen, like cobblers and pinmakers, who would agree to take them, and when they did the children were usually cruelly overworked and underfed.

The next move to help destitute children came only a few years later. In 1552 an institution called Christ's Hospital was opened in London to look after and educate some five hundred orphans. This was soon followed by similar schools in Cambridge, Ipswich, Norwich and Lincoln, mainly supported by contributions from the prosperous, new middle-class merchants.

These schools could not accommodate all the homeless, destitute children, of course. Also the standard of care and attention they gave the children varied considerably from one school to another. Nevertheless, they represented one of the first genuine attempts to help poor, needy children, and fit them to become useful, self-supporting members of the community.

56 Edward VI presenting charters to Christ's, Bridewell, and St Thomas's Hospitals before the Lord Mayor of London.

10 Games and Sports

Small children in Tudor times played much the same kind of games as they do today. Prisoner's Base, Tip Cat and Hide and Seek (called Hoop and Hide in those days) were all very popular. Other favourites were Battledore and Shuttlecock, Bowling the Hoop, and Top and Scourge (the Tudor name for playing with a top and a whip).

Another popular game with small children was Hoodman Blind. This was something like Blind Man's Buff, except that the 'blind man' had to cover his eyes with his hood. Then all the other children put knots in their own hoods, and took turns at smacking the 'blind man' until he guessed who it was who had hit him.

Ball games

There were also a large number of ball games for small children. In Nine Holes, for instance, they had to try to roll some balls into nine holes, specially cut in the ground. Stoolball was an early form of cricket, played with just one upright post for a wicket, and Bandy Ball was a very simple version of putting, or golf.

Equally popular was a game rather like Ninepins. Nine cone-shaped sticks were arranged in rows of three, and the players had to try to knock them down. Sometimes a ball was used, and the game was called Kyals or Loggats. But sometimes the players threw a piece of wood at the sticks, and then it was known as Club Kyals.

All the games mentioned so far were played by small children of all classes, although some of them, like Stoolball and Bandy Ball, were usually only played by boys. When the children grew older, however, and wanted to take part in more serious sports, the kind of pastimes they could take up depended almost entirely on their social position.

Rich boys: Hunting and jousting

Easily the most popular sport for boys from wealthy families was hunting. Most noblemen took it in turns to arrange hunting parties on their estates, and their sons joined in as soon as they were able to ride. The animals that were chiefly hunted were wild boars, hares and deers. Foxes were not hunted for pleasure. They were merely regarded as vermin, and either trapped or shot.

57 Boys playing kyals or loggats.

58   Children enjoying a picnic at a hunting party, from the 'Booke of Hunting', 1575

59   James I holding a hawk on his fist. His leather glove protected his hand from the bird's talons.

After hunting, the most popular sport among rich boys was hawking, or falconry. Poor boys were not able to take part, because the falcons were too expensive to breed and train. Even when they were trained, the falcons still needed a great deal of time and skill to be spent on them, and wealthy people nearly always employed professional falconers.

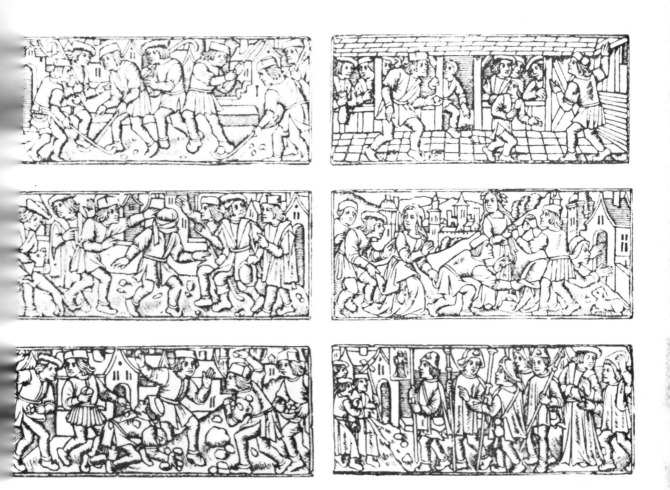

60   These illustrations from 1500 show children playing hockey, tennis, blind man's buff, oranges and lemons, snow-balling, and beating the bounds. Parishioners would beat the bounds with willow sticks on Ascension Day to preserve the limits of the parish.

The aim of hawking was to use the falcons to catch other birds. A boy would first put on a thickly padded gauntlet, and then place the falcon on his hand. (The gauntlet was to prevent the falcon digging its claws into him.) Next the boy would cover the falcon's head with a hood, so that it would not catch sight of some other bird and fly off too soon. When the boy was ready, he removed the hood, and the falcon at once soared into the air. Then it hovered over its prey for a few moments, and suddenly swooped down on it. The birds that were usually hunted were partridges, pheasants, woodcocks, wild ducks and herons, although it naturally varied a little in different parts of the country.

In early Tudor times many young noblemen liked to tilt and to joust. In fact, the boy-king, Edward VI, said that tilting was his favourite outdoor amusement. Both of these sports were originally designed to teach boys of noble families how to fight on horseback, in case they were ever called to arms, in the days before guns were invented.

In the case of tilting, a metal ring was placed on a hook about two metres above the ground. Then the horseman galloped towards it, and tried to lift the ring off the hook with his lance. The aim of jousting was for one knight to unseat another from his horse with his lance, but there was always a low fence between the two combatants, to prevent them injuring each other too seriously.

Rich boys: Tennis
In the early part of the Tudor period tennis became popular among rich young men. It was always played indoors, however, on specially constructed tennis courts. In fact, present day visitors to Hampton Court can still see the beautiful court on which Henry VIII played tennis (or paume, as it was sometimes called) as a young man.

In later Tudor times tennis was occasionally played out of doors. But it was still played only by the wealthy, who could afford all the equipment. Also girls never played, although they probably enjoyed watching, as we still have this account of a game of tennis played in the presence of Queen Elizabeth: 'About three o'clock ten of the Earl of Hertford's men hung up lines in a square grass court, in front of her Majesty's windows. They squared out the form of the court, making a cross line in the middle. Then in this square (having taken off their doublets) they played five on each side, with a small ball, to the great liking of her Highness.'

Fives also became quite popular towards the end of the Tudor period. So did a number of other games, which all more or less resembled our modern squash or racquets. They were all games for wealthy, aristocratic boys, however, because of the considerable expense of constructing the special indoor courts on which they were played.

Poor boys: Football
Far and away the most popular game with poorer boys was football. This was a much rougher game in Tudor times than it is today, however. There were few rules, no lines and no limit to the number of players in a team. In fact, someone writing at the time described a Tudor game of football as 'a friendly kind of fight'. Another writer said, 'Does not every player in a football game lie in wait for his adversary, seeking to knock him down or to punch him on the nose? Sometimes the players' necks are broken, sometimes their backs, sometimes their legs, sometimes their arms. Sometimes their arms and legs are thrust out of joint, and sometimes their noses gush with blood'.

It is hardly surprising that the government tried to discourage football. So did the guilds, who thought that apprentices took too much time off from work on account of their injuries. The clergy also disapproved of football, because boys wanted to play on Sundays; and the university authorities at Oxford banned it completely.

Poor boys: Hurling
Football was by no means the only rough and dangerous game, however. There were two other equally rough games that were both known, in different parts of the country, as hurling.

One of these games was played with a large ball made of box, yew or holly, which one writer of the period tells us was 'boiled in tallow to make it more slippery'. There were fifteen to thirty players on each side, and the aim of the game was to pick up the ball and run with it through your opponents' goal. If a player was tackled he had to pass the ball to one of his team-mates, but, as in

61 Young men improved their archery skills by shooting at the popinjay (a live bird tied to the top of a long pole).

the modern game of Rugby, he always had to pass the ball backwards.

The other game of hurling was played with curved wooden sticks, and the object was to hit a small wooden ball through the goal of the opposing team. It was, in fact, rather like hockey, except that the ball was not hit along the ground, but up through the air, which must have made the game a lot more exciting!

Poor boys: Other games

Wrestling was another sport which often led to serious injuries. So did 'cudgelling', a game for two players, each armed with a very thick, short stick. The chief aim in 'cudgelling' was to hit your opponent over the head with the stick, and points were scored whenever you made his head bleed!

Another rough game played by poorer boys was called Dun the Cart-Horse. The 'dun' was a large log of wood, which was dragged on to the village green, and set upright. Then one player shouted, 'Dun is stuck in the mire!' and this was the signal for half a dozen other players to rush forward and try to topple the log over. If they did not succeed, everyone started shouting, 'More hands! More hands!' Then all the other players rushed forward, and joined in the fun. There do not appear to have been any particular rules, except that anyone who was hit on the head by the log was said to be 'out', and no doubt with good reason!

Sports for boys of all classes

Most boys, rich and poor, liked to swim if they had the chance. There were no swimming-pools, though, so they could only swim if they lived near a river or by the sea. In those days everyone did the breast-stroke (the crawl had not been invented), and boys were given bundles of rushes to keep them afloat while they were learning.

Fishing was also enjoyed by boys, as well as girls, of all classes. People did not usually fish with a rod and line when they went out for a day's fishing for pleasure, however. They generally waded into the river with a fishing-net, or even with a wide-mouthed wicker basket, and amused themselves by trying to scoop the fish out of the water.

In early Tudor times bows and arrows were still used in warfare. But gradually archery became little more than a sport for boys, and sometimes girls, of all classes. The bows used for sport were made of hazel, ash or elm. (They were not made of yew, like the bows which had been used in earlier times on the battlefield.) The length of the bow depended on the height of the archer. The rule was that it had to be as long as the archer was tall, plus the length of the archer's foot. The best arrows were made from birch, ash and hornbeam, and a grey goose feather was traditionally used for winging the arrow.

Peaceful pastimes

The Tudor period, generally speaking, was a violent age. So it is hardly surprising that most of the games played by young people at that time were violent, too. Nevertheless, there were a certain number of gentler pastimes, like pall-mall, a game rather similar to croquet, which was very popular with the sons and daughters of wealthy families. There was also bowls, the game which, according to tradition, Sir Francis Drake (1540-1596) was playing on Plymouth Hoe when the Spanish Armada was sighted sailing up the Channel. This was popular with boys and girls of all classes in Tudor times, the poorer children playing it on the village greens, and the rich on specially constructed bowling alleys on their family estates.

Index

The numbers in **bold type** refer to the figure numbers of the illustrations